FANTASTIC CREATURES

And How To Draw Them

This book belongs to:

....

FANTASTIC CREATURES

And How To Draw Them

Kev Walker

Search Press

A QUARTO BOOK

This edition published in 2018 by
Search Press Ltd
Wellwood
North Farm Road
Tunbridge Wells
Kent TN2 3DR
United Kingdom

ISBN 978-1-78221-688-9

Conceived, edited and designed by
Quarto Publishing plc
The Old Brewery
6 Blundell Street
London N7 9BH

www.quartoknows.com

QUAR.FBHD

Editor: Claire Waite Brown
Designer: Hugh Schermuly
Art director: Emma Clayton
Publisher: Samantha Warrington

Printed in China

CONTENTS

INTRODUCTION

Modern fantasy art and literature are steeped in the folklore, myths and legends of times past, which have always been populated by strange creatures far removed from the domestic animals that share our lives. Fantastic creatures such as dragons, werewolves and vampires give us enemies to fear and hazards to overcome, while sea monsters provide a visual metaphor for the things we suspect lurk below the ocean waves.

But how do we draw these mythical creatures that we can only glimpse in our imagination? *Fantastic Creatures and How to Draw Them* answers this question by showing how fantasy artists produce their visions of strange worlds and the beasts that dwell in them. Most fantasy has a starting point in reality, so look at real animals, birds and insects and try to envisage ways of turning them into something different by distorting anatomical forms or altering scale. A cockroach is nasty enough on a small scale, but think of one as big as a house!

The book begins by suggesting where you might find ideas and inspiration for your work, and then shows you some useful techniques for a number of different drawing media. On the pages that follow the fantasy beasts are organised into six different habitats. Each entry features a finished illustration of the creature and guidelines for recreating it. The section is packed with exciting ideas, including hints on suggesting movement, ways to decide on poses and practical lessons on drawing claws, scales, teeth and other vital attributes of fantasy beasts.

There are also interactive pages for each creature, so you can copy the examples given or use the demonstrations and illustrations as a springboard for taking off into your own realm of fantasy and imagination.

Inspiration

Where do the ideas come from? This is a question most artists are asked from time to time, especially if their speciality is fantasy art, and the only real answer is 'everywhere and nowhere'. Ideas can't be summoned up to order, and often come to you when you least expect them, sometimes triggered by random visual effects such as a pattern of light on a wall. So keep your mind open, and don't rule anything out.

Architecture
Gargoyles such as this one can be found adorning buildings all over the world.

Starting point

Most fantasy art has a starting point in reality, and this is especially true of fantasy beasts – you can't create a realistic-looking creature without considering those that actually are real. Your beasts must look as though they can move, eat, hunt and do all the things that living creatures do, however strange their structure, habits and environment. So try to understand how a skeleton and layers of muscle can form the outward shape of a creature and how movement affects this shape. Zoos can be a useful place for gathering ideas, or you can use illustrated books and the Internet. Look at photographs and films of animals and insects to discover how they are constructed – you will often find that fact really is stranger than fiction.

Past and present

It's always worth looking at the work of other artists, too. Fantasy beasts have featured in art throughout history, from prehistoric cave paintings through the gargoyles of medieval times to the graphic novels and computer games of today. If you have a particular type of creature in mind, look at how other artists have approached the concept, in this book and through the ages. Don't waste time wondering how they have made the drawing, painting or sculpture; what matters is the shapes created and the reasoning behind the creation. Folklore and myth are other good sources of inspiration, and here you have a wide choice of material – all cultures have their own ideas of strange creatures, often with magical abilities.

The natural world
The earth is capable of amazing feats of destruction and renewal. Who knows what creatures might evolve with it.

Bending reality

Even if your creature is based on a real one, or a combination of several, you can give it a more fantastical appearance by changing the scale or setting it in a different environment. Creatures that are microscopic in real life can become gargantuan in your creation, or something that exists only in the sea can be transposed to another setting, becoming modified along the way. For example, a jellyfish wouldn't last long in a desert, but by taking its basic shape and giving it a rigid skeleton and a different skin surface you can create a whole new creature. And, of course, you can 'mix and mismatch', using the eyes of one creature and the ears of another. Imagine a horse with the hair of a dog and the ears and tail of a pig, for example.

Collecting visual information

When you have an idea, don't waste it; act immediately to record it. Notebooks and sketchbooks are vital, and a scrapbook is also a good idea because it provides a way of keeping interesting images you may find in magazines, newspapers or printed from the Internet, as well as scraps of material and anything else that might come in handy for the colours and textures of your creatures. Taking photos on a smartphone will help you to make visual notes of anything you may see when out and about, helping you to remember things you don't have time to sketch.

Wonders of nature
Some of the world's real animals are truly fantastical.

Inspirational records
Take frequent photographs for visual reference. You can keep them together on the relevant journal pages of this book.

PENCILS, PASTELS AND PENS

To recreate the creatures shown in this book, or produce your personal versions of them, you can use a selection of tools. Some suggestions are provided over the following pages, but you can of course use your own favourites, or whatever is handy. The techniques associated with each medium are shown on pages 12–17.

Pencils and erasers

Pencils are made in different grades, H denoting soft and B standing for black. There are several different types of erasers, but avoid very hard ones because they leave greasy smears and can damage the surface of the paper.

Erasers
A white plastic eraser is best for removing large areas of pencil. Remove debris with a soft brush before continuing with the drawing. A kneaded eraser can be pulled to a fine point to remove small areas and produce highlights.

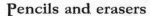

Mechanical pencil
A useful alternative to wood-cased pencils because you can change the lead to suit your purpose.

Grades of pencil
HB is in the middle of the range, and is a good all-rounder; 2B, 4B and below are better for sketchy or expressive work.

Coloured pencils

Coloured pencils are popular with illustrators, especially for detailed work, but the softer ones can also be blended for broader effects. They are made in a huge range of colours, but can also be bought in boxed sets of 12 or more.

Chalky coloured pencils
These can be blended for soft effects by rubbing with a blending stick (see right) or a clean finger.

Waxy coloured pencils
These are excellent for detail, but less easy to blend than chalky pencils. Both types can be mixed on the paper surface by laying one colour over another.

Pastels and pastel pencils

Soft pastels, which crumble and smudge easily, are not well suited to detailed illustration work, and they also make a great deal of mess, requiring a dedicated work space – or a large dust sheet. Hard pastels and pastel pencils are more manageable and good for drawing to define detail and create areas of texture.

Hard pastels
These are good for covering large areas such as backgrounds because they can be used on their sides.

Pastel pencils
Harder than the paper-wrapped pastels, but softer than coloured pencils, these are easy to blend.

Blending stick
Sometimes called a torchon, use this implement for blending small areas of pastel or coloured pencil.

Pen and ink

Drawing with a pen allows you to build up very fine detail and has the added advantage of not smudging. Pens and inks are made in a wide range of colours, so you can complete a whole drawing with inks.

Fountain pen
Metal-nibbed pen with ink cartridge. Delivers a constant flow of ink.

Fibre-tip pens
Available in different point sizes and a range of colours, these make a more mechanical line than metal-nibbed pens.

India ink
Traditional ink for use with dip pens.

Ballpoint and rollerball pens
Inexpensive and useful drawing implements, although available only in a limited point size. Rollerballs tend to be slightly wetter than ballpoints.

Dip pen
Pen holder with interchangeable nibs, allowing you to make a variety of different lines. These pens are slow to use because they must be charged with ink after each stroke.

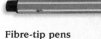

DRAWING TECHNIQUES

One of the best things about drawing is that you never stop learning. Some artists specialise in only one medium, pushing it to its limits; others find the huge variety available as exciting as the vision they are attempting to recreate. There is always something new to try, and don't forget that most of the media can be used on their own or combined with others, as can the range of techniques. So carry out your own experiments until you find a way of working that you are comfortable with, allowing you to get down on paper the image you have in your head.

Graphite pencils

The ordinary 'lead' pencil may seem a mundane implement, but the invention of the graphite pencil in the sixteenth century revolutionised drawing as artists quickly recognised its superiority over earlier drawing tools. Graphite pencils are probably the most versatile drawing instruments you will ever possess, so never underestimate them. They can provide almost endless variations of line and tonal quality, and are made in a range of grades from very hard to very soft. Standard drawing pencils are encased in wood, but you can also buy just the graphite in the form of a thick stick, ideal for creating large areas of tone by using the side of the stick rather than the point.

Hatching
In this method, tones are built up with strokes following roughly the same direction. Darker shades are achieved by going over previous layers with heavier strokes.

Cross-hatching
Hatching lines are laid first, and then another set of lines is added, crossing over the first. The denser and closer together the lines, the darker the tone.

Scribble
Rather than making single strokes, keep the pencil on the paper all the time, using a loose zigzagging motion. Create dark and light tones by adjusting the pressure and overlaying.

Shading
Solid areas of tone and soft gradations can be created by using close-together lines made with a blunt pencil. You can soften the gradations even further by rubbing with a finger to blend the lines.

Eraser shading
Tones can be lightened and highlights achieved by lifting out pencil marks with a kneaded eraser moulded to a point. Use either a stroking or stippling motion depending on the desired effect.

Pencil grades
The range of tones can be increased by using different grades of pencil: hard for light areas and soft for dark ones. Lay the soft pencils over the hard ones, or use different grades for each area of a drawing.

Use this page to practise pencil techniques.

13

Coloured pencils

Several different types of coloured pencil are available, some waxy and others chalky (and thus easier to blend). If possible, try them out before using to discover which best suit your purpose – they are available individually as well as in sets.

Blending by hatching
By using different coloured pencils and making hatching strokes in a uniform direction, you can create colour changes and blends.

Blending by cross-hatching
This method is excellent for delicate shading and colour transitions. Variations in colour strength can be created by changing the layers of the strokes and overlapping them at different angles.

Scribble blending
This method, which is basically the same as scribble pencil drawing (see page 12), can give a much denser and more textural shading and colouring effect. Colours are usually worked from light to dark.

Rubbing
Blending coloured pencil by rubbing with a cotton bud, a blending stick or your fingers creates soft, blurred effects. The chalkier the coloured pencil, the easier this is to do.

Frottage
Placing the drawing paper on top of a flat, textured surface, such as a piece of loosely woven fabric, and shading with the coloured pencils allows the underlying texture or pattern to come through.

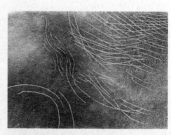

Impressing
If you indent the paper with a suitable tool, then draw over it, the indented lines will remain white. Here, a blunted compass point has been used to create a pattern of fine lines.

Use this page to practise coloured pencil techniques.

Drawing with ink

Drawing with ink is the oldest of all drawing methods.
A wide variety of drawing pens are available, from dip pens
with interchangeable nibs to many different types of reservoir
pens, which contain their own inks. As with all drawing,
experimentation is the key, since all pens act and feel differently
in your hand. Fibre-tip pens deliver a constant flow of ink;
traditional metal-nibbed pens give more variation in line. Ink
drawings can't be corrected later, so experiment with a variety
of implements to discover the marks they make before using
inks for a finished drawing.

Nibbed pen
A nibbed pen with its own ink
cartridge (fountain pen) can be
used to produce very detailed and
tight drawings or loose expressive
sketches. The consistent flow of
ink can make it easier to control
than a dip pen.

Dip pen
A dip pen has to be repeatedly
dipped into the ink, resulting in
more uneven lines, but the drawing
style can be scratchy and energetic.
Nibs are available in assorted
shapes and sizes.

Fine-point marker
These pens deliver a consistent and
rather mechanical line, although
drawing on a soft surface can help
create some variation. Very dense
cross-hatching can be made with
these pens.

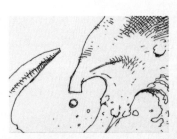

Rapidograph
Available in several point sizes,
rapidographs are primarily used
for technical drawing, but can be
used to sketch and are especially
useful for creating quirky, scratchy
lines. The ink is waterproof and the
lines constant.

Coloured line
Drawing pens are made in a
variety of colours, as are drawing
inks. Using a series of coloured
lines, either with a fine-point
marker or a nibbed pen, can create
a range of different effects and
coloured surface textures.

Ballpoint pen
These everyday implements are
excellent for quick, spontaneous
sketching or for working into
more complicated drawings in
conjunction with other pens. Even
black ballpoints can vary in shade,
some creating quite grey lines,
as in this case.

Use this page to practise your technique.

NIGHT BEASTS

Many known and unknown beasts use the cover of darkness to hide their activities. Nocturnal creatures can be quiet and meek or predatory and dangerous, and there are plenty of sources of inspiration you could turn to.

Finding inspiration

Some creatures, although fairly harmless in reality, conjure up fear by virtue of their nocturnal activities. Most bats are gentle, passive creatures, but their reputation is just the opposite.

Night beasts can be inspired by darkness in general, not just at nighttime. Stormy weather conjures up thoughts of dark and powerful forces at work.

Sketch skeletons in order to build up your physique-drawing skills. Your local museum will have some for you to look at.

Creatures that shed their skins, or undergo a complete metamorphosis, can really stir the imagination, offering two fantasy beasts in one.

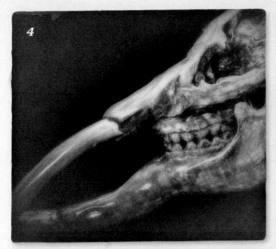

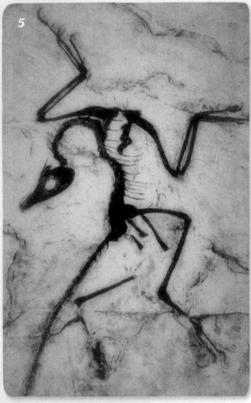

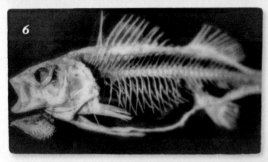

Gather your own sources of inspiration for night beasts here. Attach photos and make sketches, considering how you might translate aspects to your fantasy creations.

NIGHT ELEMENTAL

The night elemental is a magical creature drawn from the dark matter of night. It can manifest itself in many forms, but favours characteristics taken from creatures associated with the night. This incarnation displays elements of cats, bats and owls.

The night elemental can become a creature as big as 4.5 metres (15 feet) long. Its appearance varies as it takes on the characteristics of the animal form it adopts, but it can always be recognised by the starlight sparkling in its depths. It is found in the darkest of night shadows, and its appearance often coincides with the moon entering its transition phase, from waning to waxing.

HUMAN HAND

BAT WING

Wing and claw detail
By exaggerating the claws, fur and ragged edges of the bat wing, you can add a greater sense of menace.

Emerging from cloud
The night elemental forms from the dark shadows of a moonlit cloud, and it begins to adopt the form of the night creatures whose qualities it embodies.

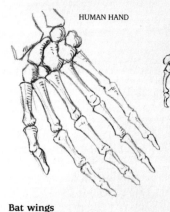

Bat wings
When drawing a creature with bat wings, note the similarity in bone structure between a human hand and that of the bat's wing.

This night elemental has been coloured using acrylic paints and, for extra sparkle, iridescent acrylic inks.

FANTASY FEATHERS

The contrast between these two feather sketches illustrates the difference between a realistic and imaginative approach. The exaggeration of the feather form makes the second drawing more exciting and dramatic.

Figure constuction

The pencil construction shows how the elements of the component creatures are brought together.

Now draw your own night elementals.

Exaggeration of reality
Here you can see the
contrast between a straight
representation of an owl
and one benefiting from
the artist's exaggeration,
which adds a greater sense
of viciousness and evil.

NIGHT DRAGON

The dragon is one of the oldest mythological creatures. It has a widespread history, appearing in the traditions of virtually all countries and continents back to the beginning of time.

The form of the dragon is defined by its limbs, which can allude to the environment in which it lives – a water dragon, for example, may not need limbs at all. Other attributes, such as the neck length and whether it has wings or fire-breathing abilities, are the artist's personal choice.

Dragon pose
The dragon pose is based on a symmetrical curved line.

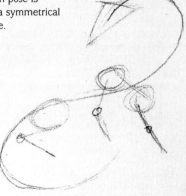

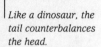

Like a dinosaur, the tail counterbalances the head.

The more complicated the curve, the more action-packed the pose.

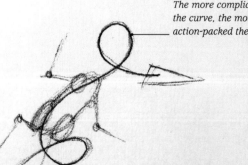

Dragon forms
Dragon forms are defined by the limbs.

Large hindquarters and large forelimbs. The wings are optional.

Dragon's nature

A dragon can be passive or aggressive, so the pose is extremely important.

Aggressive
The mouth is open and roaring, the neck is arched and the arms and legs are ready for action.

Passive
The mouth is closed, the neck relaxed, the wings closed and the arms and legs are firmly on the ground.

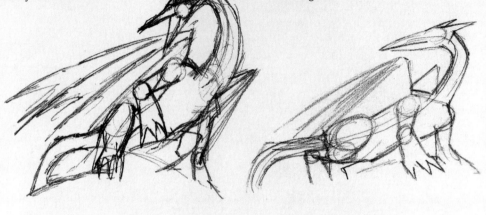

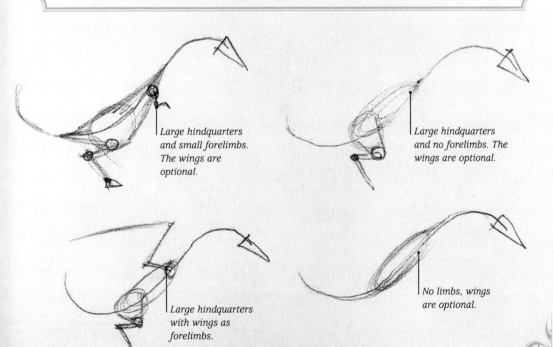

Large hindquarters and small forelimbs. The wings are optional.

Large hindquarters and no forelimbs. The wings are optional.

Large hindquarters with wings as forelimbs.

No limbs, wings are optional.

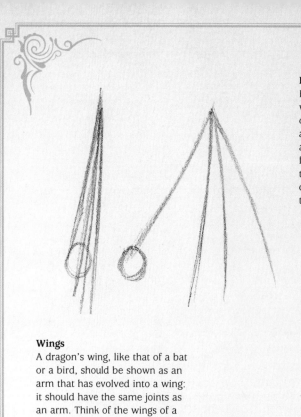

Foreshortening

Foreshortening a flat shape, like a dragon's wing, will give the impression of it being placed at an oblique angle to the viewer. Draw the full shape on a small piece of paper, then tilt it in at the required angle and copy what you see. When filling out the form, remember that lines and shapes become closer together towards the back, so start with the part closest to you, then position the further shapes behind those at the front.

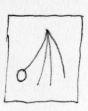

FLAT SHAPE

FORESHORTENED SHAPE

Wings

A dragon's wing, like that of a bat or a bird, should be shown as an arm that has evolved into a wing: it should have the same joints as an arm. Think of the wings of a dragon as a built-in hang-glider.

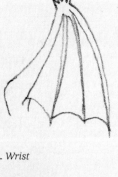

Vestigial

Wrist

Fingers

Elbow

Shoulder

Evolution of the wing

The fingers have no joints, which is necessary in order to tighten the skin membrane between them. The thumb becomes vestigial – a primary horn, with other growths clustering around it. The fingers themselves would be light, and probably made of cartilage in order to be flexible.

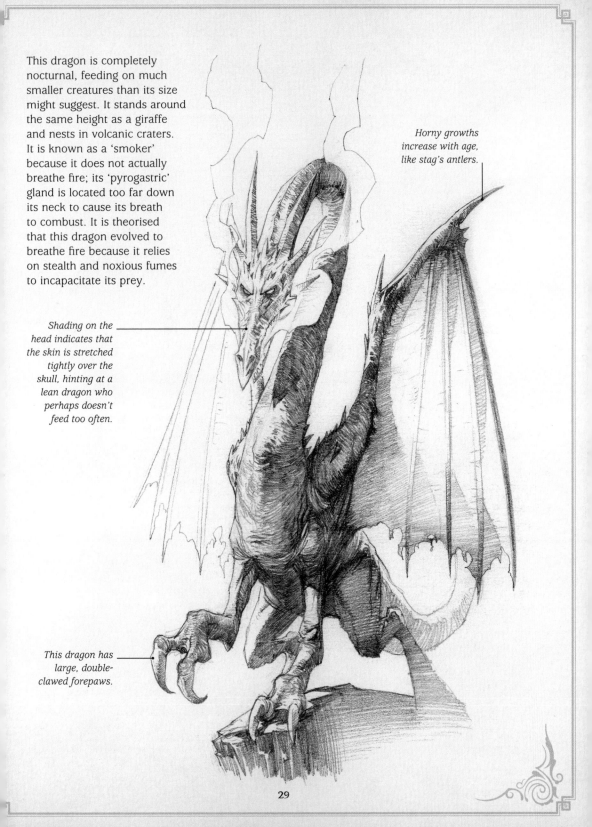

This dragon is completely nocturnal, feeding on much smaller creatures than its size might suggest. It stands around the same height as a giraffe and nests in volcanic craters. It is known as a 'smoker' because it does not actually breathe fire; its 'pyrogastric' gland is located too far down its neck to cause its breath to combust. It is theorised that this dragon evolved to breathe fire because it relies on stealth and noxious fumes to incapacitate its prey.

Horny growths increase with age, like stag's antlers.

Shading on the head indicates that the skin is stretched tightly over the skull, hinting at a lean dragon who perhaps doesn't feed too often.

This dragon has large, double-clawed forepaws.

Now draw your own night dragons.

VAMPIRE

Vampire stories date back thousands of years
and exist in most cultures around the world.
Vampire myths arrived in the West, through
Eastern Europe, with travelling merchants
selling their wares and telling tales of distant
lands. Today, vampire stories still hold true
to those old Eastern European tales of blood-
drinking nocturnal beings who have returned
from the dead, but many of the familiar ideas
– the wearing of capes, having no reflection,
and morphing into bats – are modern
inventions.

This creature is completely nocturnal, exhibiting
an extreme photosensitivity. It feeds principally
on the blood of other warm-blooded mammals
in order to alleviate a natural anemia. This diet
makes the vampire very skinny. The vampiric
condition can be passed to humans via its
bite, giving rise to similar feeding habits
among sufferers.

Garlic contains an enzyme that causes an
extreme reaction in both purebred vampires
and contaminated humans, similar to that
caused by poison ivy or nettles.

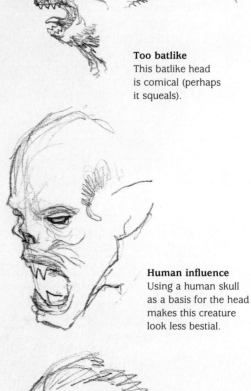

Too batlike
This batlike head
is comical (perhaps
it squeals).

Human influence
Using a human skull
as a basis for the head
makes this creature
look less bestial.

Drawing a skull
The basic shape of
a human skull is
circular, with the
lower jaw hanging
off the lower front.

*Following the basic
shape, you can
distort a creature's
skull in any direction.*

A mind of its own
After several sketches, the head begins
to take on a shape of its own.

The fangs are vital for the vampire's survival.

Construction

Explore the creature's construction. Front or side views are better at this stage because they help to build up a mental picture of the form. Begin with pale lines and use circles to represent the main joints.

Refining

Stretch or shrink the distance between joints to change the creature's form. Notice the shortened distance between the neck and shoulders, creating a hunched effect. The spine is short in comparison with the upper leg, and the forearms are long.

Omitting the thumb and giving the creature a withered little finger, like the vestigial toe on a dog's paw, makes the creature more animalistic.

You may want to develop your creature once you have perfected its design. This vampire has been coloured with pale washes of acrylic paint.

Now draw your own vampires.

Drawing claws

Claws are just long, sharp finger- or toenails, with the same physiological make-up. Think about what you want the claws to say about your creature. These examples are fundamentally the same, but subtle differences can make big changes to the end result.

WEREWOLF

The werewolf has been used as a symbol of humankind's inner struggle with their own animalistic tendencies for centuries. This duality is what you are attempting to depict – human and beast in the same form.

A werewolf should be able to stand upright on two legs and have opposable thumbs; otherwise, it will be too animalistic and less of a monster. However, running on all fours is faster, so the arms and legs should be of similar lengths to facilitate an easy transition between being on two legs and on all four, like a primate.

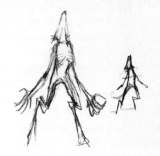

Classic pose
Howling at the moon. This shows exaggerated proportions.

Torque
Hunched back hints at muscular tension, and power ready to be unleashed, like a sprinter on the blocks.

Could the wolf grow out of the human torso?
This would require a big tail to counterbalance the rest of its body.

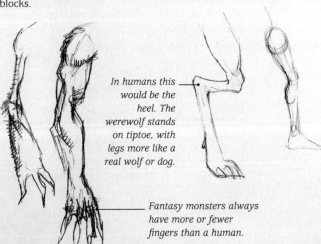

In humans this would be the heel. The werewolf stands on tiptoe, with legs more like a real wolf or dog.

The ratlike werewolf
This is not out of the question, but rodents have different natures from wolves.

Fantasy monsters always have more or fewer fingers than a human.

Doglike
Your creation doesn't need to have wolfish features. You could go for more of a doglike look.

Wolf as human
With lower ears, brow and cheeks, this version looks monkeyish and baboonlike.

Fairy-tale wolf
With a wolf face, long snout and shaggy fur, this sketch depicts the typical fairy-tale wolf.

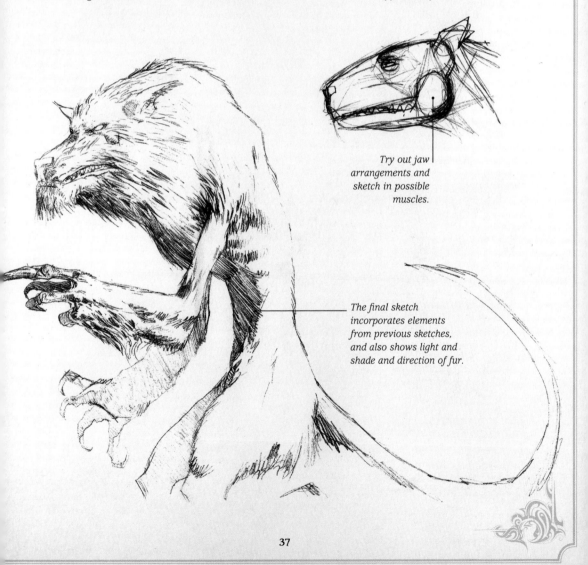

Try out jaw arrangements and sketch in possible muscles.

The final sketch incorporates elements from previous sketches, and also shows light and shade and direction of fur.

Now draw your own werewolves.

Why not try to
capture the werewolf
mid-transformation?

DEMON

Demons have taken many forms over the centuries, but are traditionally seen as evil spirits or devils, though they can sometimes be good.

Evil demons flourish in densely populated but poor areas, and can usually be found infesting waste and landfill sites or amid derelict human habitation. They feed in a unique manner, draining bioelectric energy from whatever life-form happens to cross their path. Although their feeding is not fatal in itself, it often leaves their victims weak and open to attack from disease, causing psychological changes such as mood swings, torpor and (in extreme cases) manic depression. The demon has a skeleton that grows throughout its life, developing random extrusions and bony spurs.

Creating form
This demon has basic goatlike features – horns and a pointed head. The legs too resemble the hind legs of a goat. Note the reverse foot.

Too goatlike
A completely goatlike demon could seem too passive and nonthreatening, so you need to humanise the features.

Traditional view
This traditional demon, taken from pre-Christian myth, is the ancient Greek god Pan, with half-human, half-goat features.

Scribble technique
An amorphous design like this is best sketched using the scribble technique: shapes are refined by increasing layers of pencil detail.

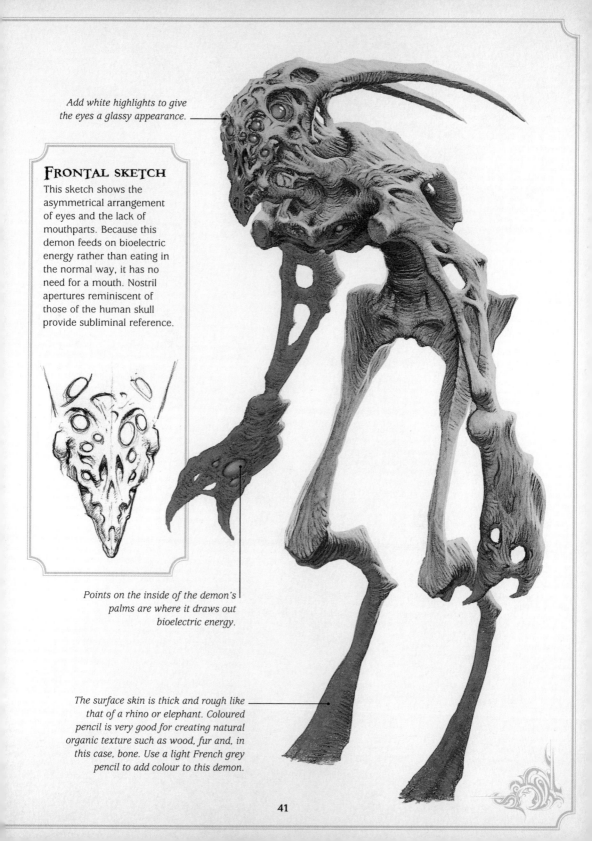

Add white highlights to give
the eyes a glassy appearance.

FRONTAL SKETCH

This sketch shows the
asymmetrical arrangement
of eyes and the lack of
mouthparts. Because this
demon feeds on bioelectric
energy rather than eating in
the normal way, it has no
need for a mouth. Nostril
apertures reminiscent of
those of the human skull
provide subliminal reference.

Points on the inside of the demon's
palms are where it draws out
bioelectric energy.

The surface skin is thick and rough like
that of a rhino or elephant. Coloured
pencil is very good for creating natural
organic texture such as wood, fur and, in
this case, bone. Use a light French grey
pencil to add colour to this demon.

Now draw your own demons.

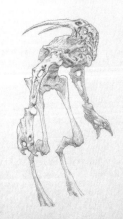

SEA BEASTS

The ocean is full of curious creatures. A trip to an aquarium or natural history museum could be all it takes to give you an idea for a sea-based beast. Or you could try reading old stories about sea serpents.

Finding inspiration

The plant life of the ocean is often as colourful and lively as the animal life.

Sharks are one of the longest surviving predators on the planet, with evidence of their existence dating back 430 million years. Their sleek, streamlined bodies help them swim without using a lot of energy. This is important because they never really sleep, and most of them never stop swimming.

Look for common characteristics in real ocean dwellers and try to use some of them in your fantasy creatures.

Squid and octopi are among nature's strangest looking creatures. They could even be straight out of the realm of fantasy.

Fig. 1: Nautilus
Fig. 2: Seaweed
Fig. 3: Anemone
Fig. 4: Octopus
Fig. 5: Scorpionfish
Fig. 6: Great white shark
Fig. 7: Leafy sea dragon

Use these pages to collect your own examples of inspiration for sea beasts, from nature, reference books and the internet. Make notes to help you recall what it is that drew you to particular images, and how you might use this in your fantasy art.

SEA ELEMENTAL

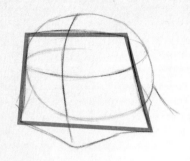

Like the mighty ocean in which it lives, the sea elemental is powerful, fast and easily provoked. The elemental's webbed hands and massive tail allow it to swim with amazing speed; its blue-green colouring and plantlike hair make it difficult to spot when it wishes to go undetected.

While sometimes willing to help humans lost at sea, the sea elemental is just as likely to capsize an unfortunate boat on a whim. Its wrath can be great when confronting human-made objects it considers harmful to its realm, such as commercial whalers or leaking oil tankers. By thrashing its mighty tail, the sea elemental can usually generate waves large enough to scuttle any vessel, and its sharp claws and amazing strength enable it to punch a hole in most ships.

This sea elemental has been given a mysterious and alien look by incorporating elements from both sea plants and sea creatures. However, by adding humanlike arms and a vaguely human head, you can make sure the viewer knows it is intelligent and probably able to communicate.

Head shape
The head can be made from simple shapes. It is flatter than a human head and needs a lot of space for the large eyes and mouth. Starting with a rough trapezoid with the bottom larger than the top, as shown here, can help you get the right shape.

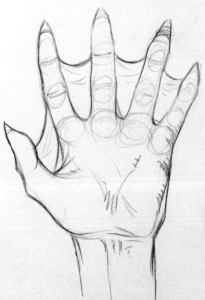

Webbed fingers
When pushing against the water, the webbed fingers serve much the same purpose as a fish's tail, generating force for locomotion. When slicing through the water they drag less than human fingers.

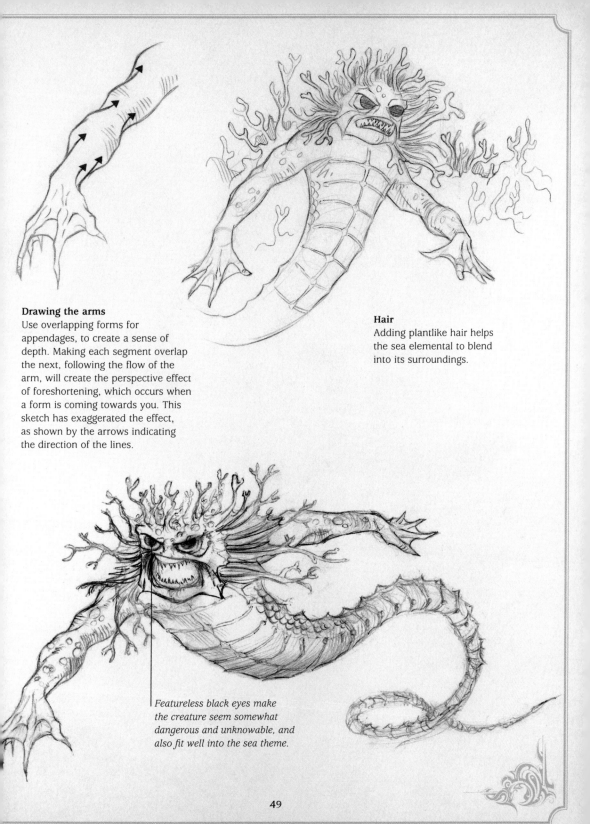

Drawing the arms
Use overlapping forms for appendages, to create a sense of depth. Making each segment overlap the next, following the flow of the arm, will create the perspective effect of foreshortening, which occurs when a form is coming towards you. This sketch has exaggerated the effect, as shown by the arrows indicating the direction of the lines.

Hair
Adding plantlike hair helps the sea elemental to blend into its surroundings.

Featureless black eyes make the creature seem somewhat dangerous and unknowable, and also fit well into the sea theme.

Now draw your own sea elementals.

Drawing scales
Scales can be difficult to draw. This
two-step process will help you get
them right every time.

SEA DRAGON

This dragon is the classic sea serpent much dreaded by sailors. Fear of these creatures was at its height in the fifteenth century when Western explorers were trying to reach the East. At the time, many people believed the world was flat and that ships would sail until they fell off the end of the Earth. Maps with uncharted waters were marked 'Here be dragons'.

The sea dragon is related to the swamp dragon but can survive in both fresh and saltwater environments, and to greater depths. Like its most famous relative, the Loch Ness Monster, it is rarely seen above water.

The sea dragon is a fiercely territorial creature and has been known to attack submarines at depth. It has a voracious appetite and feeds on large aquatic creatures.

Open or closed
With large or long teeth, leave bigger gaps between them in order for the mouth to close fully, except when a character has lips (like an ape or human) that conceal the teeth inside the mouthparts.

LIGHTING A TRANSPARENT OBJECT

A conventional tooth is opaque, darkening towards the base.

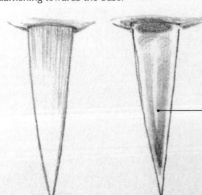

An overhead light source inverts light within the crystal ball, so that the darker area is closer to the light. There is still a highlight on the outside because the object is shiny, and even though transparent, it casts a shadow.

A translucent or transparent tooth, such as a sea dragon might have, acts more like a lens or the crystal ball shown right.

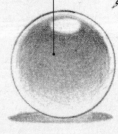

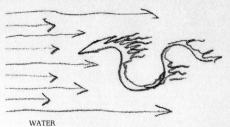

WATER

The illusion of movement
Create a sense of movement that acknowledges the structure and behaviour of the creature. The sea dragon has no limbs, and its insubstantial winglike fins could not possibly move such a large creature on their own. Giving it an undulating shape suggests that it moves through the water rather like an eel.

The direction of the water acting on this sea dragon is opposite to the direction in which it is travelling. The sense of movement is increased by making the leafy tendrils on the fins recede behind it, as though trailing in the water.

Now draw your own sea dragons.

CHARACTER SKETCHES

KRAKEN

The kraken is a fearsome sea monster, originating in stories from Norway in the twelfth century. According to legend, this creature, often described as being the size of a small island, could wrap its arms around the hull of a ship and capsize it.

The kraken of these stories could have been what we now know as the giant squid. Giant squid have not been seen that often, and little is known of their habits, but their existence is accepted. They are not the size of a small island, but they are large enough to wrestle with a sperm whale and have even been known to attack ships.

Krakens tend to exist in colder seas; they use the hornlike shell on their heads to break free from the ice that traps them. Their arms are covered in suckers and sharp rotating hooks.

Basic form
The kraken is made of several shapes: the mantle, the cylindrical body, the shell, the head and its many tentacles. Loose lines show the creature's sinuous nature. While these drawings have been rendered digitally, you can practise the shapes just as well with pencil or pen.

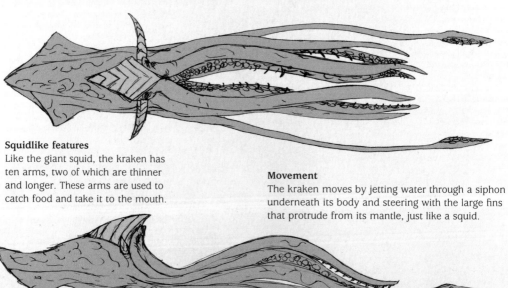

Squidlike features
Like the giant squid, the kraken has ten arms, two of which are thinner and longer. These arms are used to catch food and take it to the mouth.

Movement
The kraken moves by jetting water through a siphon underneath its body and steering with the large fins that protrude from its mantle, just like a squid.

Eyes front
The kraken's eyes are similarly positioned to those of an octopus. The horn on its head is inspired by the shells of the long-extinct belemnite.

Feeding time
The five pairs of arms surround the kraken's strong beak. The arms can trap big prey and draw it into the creature's large mouth.

The hooks on the kraken's arms are like those of the colossal squid, the biggest species of squid in the ocean.

Once you have drawn your kraken you might choose to render and colour it digitally, as has been done here.

Now draw your own krakens.

MER-CREATURE

The mer-creature is a hybrid of myths and folklore, combining elements of mermaids and other sea creatures (such as selkies and the sirens of ancient Greek myth).

The mermaid was regarded as a natural creature rather than one of supernatural origins, and was supposed to lure sailors to their deaths on shallow rocks by the power of its singing. Belief in the existence of mermaids continued until relatively recently. Indeed, so powerful has been the belief in mer-creatures that fishing communities in southwest England claimed to have persons of mermaid or merman descent living among them, people with special powers and an affinity with the sea.

MARINE MOTION

Marine mammals, such as dolphins, whales and seals, move through the water using a vertical motion.

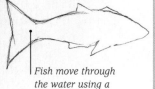

Fish move through the water using a sideways motion.

Giving the mer-creature a mammalian tail makes it look less fishlike.

Sinewy form
A long sinewy shape suggests a creature that is at home in water.

Eyelids
Fish don't have eyelids, but the mer-creature is a mammal–fish hybrid, so it could be given more human eyes. It depends on which direction you want the design to go; eyelids might swing it too far in the mammalian direction.

Face development
Large fish eyes and platelike shapes on the face are similar to those of fish.

Thin fleshy membranes on the creature's head mimic seaweed and act as camouflage.

Large gills line the creature's throat and hide any musculature on the neck.

61

Now draw your own mer-creatures.

GIANT VIPERFISH

The viperfish is a large, fast and powerful predator. This solitary beast usually hunts in the depths of the oceans, but sometimes ventures closer to shore if food is short.

The viperfish can grow up to 4 metres (13 feet) long, and weigh some 20 kilos (44 pounds), but despite its size it is rarely seen, striking unexpectedly and leaving no signs of either itself or its victim.

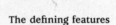

The defining features
The viperfish claims its name from the large teeth that protrude from its jaws. There are two large upper and two large lower teeth, which somewhat resemble the fangs of a viper.

Eye detail
The giant viperfish has large eyes, allowing it to see in the dark, murky waters of the ocean.

Large fins help the giant viperfish to swim at speeds exceeding 100 kilometres (60 miles) per hour.

Curved form
When drawing your viperfish use lots of S-shaped curves and overlap shapes to give your design depth.

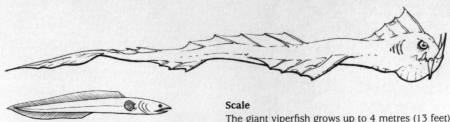

Scale
The giant viperfish grows up to 4 metres (13 feet) long, roughly three times the length of an average conger eel, which is about 1.5 metres (4½ feet).

If you choose to colour your viperfish, start with two basic colours – here red and green – then introduce subtle variations; for example, hues of blue and purple for shadows and yellow in the highlights.

Now draw your own giant viperfish.

Pencil shading
Use some of the pencil
techniques detailed on
page 12 to create form.

DESERT BEASTS

On the surface the desert may seem dry and dull, but dig a little and you'll find a wealth of creatures and stories to inspire you. Think about what could survive and evolve in such a climate.

Finding inspiration

When thinking about your fantasy beasts, use the physiology of real creatures to get you started. For example, camels, known as 'ships of the desert', have evolved physiologically to cope with both heat and dehydration.

The *Moloch* lizard is a real animal, but it looks supernatural. It is covered with thornlike spines, giving rise to the alternative name, 'thorny devil'.

Scorpions are highly dangerous creatures, but their segmented bodies make them fun to draw.

Visit a natural history museum to practise drawing skulls and bones, and you'll soon get to grips with the basic shapes.

Fig. 1: Scorpion
Fig. 2: Cattle skull
Fig. 3: Camels
Fig. 4: Sand viper
Fig. 5: Antlion larva
Fig. 6: *Moloch* lizard

Gather your own sources of inspiration for desert beasts here. Make a note of what you like about each image and consider how you might translate these characteristics to your own desert beasts.

DESERT ELEMENTAL

The desert elemental is made entirely of sand, which it can make harder or softer at will and turn into any shape it wishes. Most often, the desert elemental appears as nothing more than a tract of desert sand, indistinguishable from its surroundings. When angered or disturbed, it will rise up from the desert floor in humanoid form.

The desert elemental's motion is like a wave on the ocean, sliding from one area to another. This process can be terrifyingly fast, allowing it to travel at more than 100 kilometres (60 miles) per hour. However, because of its sandy make-up, the elemental can only exist in the desert.

This elemental's internal temperature is quite hot – 80–90°C (175–195°F). This gives it ominous glowing eyes and means sure death

for any living beings it might ingest, either by putting them in its mouth or by simply enveloping them in sand. If any human caravan is unfortunate enough to stumble on this creature, it will be swallowed up in its massive sand swell, never to be seen again. Its sense of touch is especially acute, because each grain of sand that makes up its body acts like a nerve ending.

Curving body
A curved, elongated body can be created from a series of short cylinders, as pictured here. By putting them together at different angles, the feeling of a very solid yet curved body can be achieved.

Scale
To show that your creature is large, place it next to a known object, such as a tree or house, to indicate scale. Compare these sketches. In the first, the beast could be any size, but in the second picture it is clear that it's a marauding giant.

When the desert elemental appears in humanoid form it can rise up to hundreds of metres (yards) high, using as much of the surrounding sand as it wishes to create a temporary body.

The detail of sand falling from your creature gives the impression of a being made from a loose conglomeration of material.

Now draw your own desert elementals.

DESERT DRAGON

The desert dragon is similar in look to the Komodo lizard, the largest lizard on the planet. Rather than scales, this dragon has densely wrinkled skin similar to that of a rhino or elephant.

Although this dragon is winged, it is really too heavy for sustained flight. It tends to use its wings to swoop down on its prey from large rocky cliffs and canyons. It inhabits arid desert canyons and mountainous regions; its main prey are sheep, goats and cattle.

The desert dragon is a fire-breather, but it does so only on rare occasions – for defence, or during the nights of the mating season, when the female dragons are drawn to the most impressive fire-breathing displays.

Heads
Dragon heads can be formed from a loose triangle, or a cone if seen in perspective.

The purpose of the long, pointed face is to make dragons more aerodynamic. The same principle applies to water-based dragons.

The skull follows the same drawing principles as any other creature. Use circles to show where the brain casing is situated. For the jawbone, as with other features of dragons, look to dinosaurs for inspiration.

A long, pointed head makes a dragon look sleek, cunning, sinewy and more threatening.

A short, blunt head will seldom work because it tends to make a dragon appear stupid, docile, heavy or unthreatening – rather tortoiselike, no matter how many horns and teeth you add.

Use soft pencil for medium-toned shading and to establish the main shapes.

Now draw your own desert dragons.

CHARACTER SKETCHES

SPHINX

In Greek mythology the sphinx, a creature with the head of a woman and the body of a lion, was the winged monster of Thebes. She was a curse sent by the gods, and allowed no one either to leave or enter the city. In Egypt there are numerous sphinxes, usually with human heads but sometimes with those of other animals. The Great Sphinx of Giza is a famous example of this creature. This colossal statue is a national symbol of Egypt and one of the world's best-known ancient monuments.

The Egyptian sphinx assumes the role of guardian, guarding the long-lost treasures of the pharaohs' tombs, which have been hidden beneath the desert sand for thousands of years.

The huge, muscular lion's body and vast wings of a sphinx make it a powerful creature that can travel over land or through the air at lightning speeds. Sphinxes are very intelligent and often ask riddles. They are proud and arrogant, and definitely not to be toyed with.

Drawing the paw
Notice how the two middle claws are set slightly forward, like those of a real lion.

Drawing the eyes
Solid black lines surround the oval eye shape to give that distinctive Egyptian look.

Influence and inspiration
A sphinx has the body of a lion, the wings of an eagle and the head of a human. Reference the component animals to create the form.

For the feathers, start with oval shapes and then add diagonal lines for detail. The feathers overlap each other.

For the lion's coat, draw lines moving in the same general direction but with some variation in length and angle to give a less uniform effect.

Egyptian influence
The sphinx traditionally wears an Egyptian headdress.

Gather the shapes
Begin creating your sphinx by drawing a rough outline, before gradually building up details.

You could colour your sphinx with pastels, pencils or digitally. Fill in the different areas with block colours, then build up the form by adding shadows and highlights. Use different mark-making techniques to help define the various textures of fur, feathers and metal.

Now draw your own sphinx creations.

Walk like a lion

A sphinx walks with its wings folded down. When a lion walks, the two legs on one side of its body move together, while those on the other side move apart.

MINOTAUR

The Minotaur has its roots in Greek mythology. This monster was the offspring of Queen Pasiphae, wife of King Minos of Crete, and a beautiful white bull — with whom the gods forced her to become infatuated, as a punishment for her husband's refusal to sacrifice it to Poseidon. King Minos kept the Minotaur trapped within a labyrinth, feeding him with human sacrifices until he was eventually slain by the hero Theseus.

Although this minotaur is a human–bovine hybrid, it is less human than the original mythical beast. The humanoid appearance comes from the presence of ancient protohuman genes, perhaps Neanderthal or even earlier. These genes are recessive, so minotaurs are a doomed species, and over generations the humanoid characteristics have disappeared as the dominant bovine traits asserted themselves.

Hunch
The hunched pose hints at a heavy, lumbering gait, like that of a bull.

Horn shapes
Although the bull features are all-important, there are as many types of horns as there are cattle, so experiment. The shape of the horns can decide the character as much as anything else.

Drawing hands
When drawing hands, look at your own hand as a starting point.

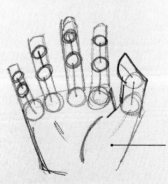

Big thick fingers make a character seem strong, but there is no room for the smallest finger.

This basic structure can be altered to suit your design.

CREATING HAND DETAIL

The use of wrinkles can indicate elasticity, suppleness and flexibility. Fewer wrinkles indicate more flexibility.

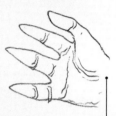

A hand without surface detail, like any part of a beast, can look like it's made of rubber.

The same hand with added wrinkles simply makes the skin look puffy and bloated because the proportions are still the same. Fat and chunky shapes mean there is still a lot of moisture in the body.

A black coloured pencil can be used to darken areas up to the waist and for the arm in the foreground.

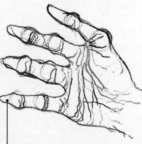

When a creature ages, it can lose body moisture and fatty tissue, especially around the joints. Major joints should be exaggerated in old, dry or starving creatures. Wrinkles should be deepened; lines always show more clearly on dry skin.

Now draw your own minotaurs.

Light from directly above

Light low and to the rear

Light from directly beneath

Lighting
A light source seemingly in the same position can be made to assume a different point in space by the addition of a shadow.

SANDWALKER

It is on the darkest, coldest nights that Bedouin tribes of the desert draw closer to the campfire and talk in whispers of the strange and fearsome creatures that stalk the dunes. Most feared among these is the sandwalker.

Rumour tells of the way in which these creatures bury themselves beneath the dunes, moving silently through the sand and then emerging from the desert floor to fall upon their victims with a frenzied attack of venomous tail, rending claw and snapping beak. Only the faint impression of crablike tracks provides irrefutable evidence that the sandwalker has been.

For fantastical beasts such as this, it is advisable to use real-world reference material. This beast combines elements of crab, scorpion and predatory birds.

Rough character
A quickly executed drawing using broad-nibbed markers establishes the fundamental characteristics of the monster. Many of these quick illustrations can be created to develop the creature's form.

Various elements
Make sketches to define the look of the various elements that combine to make up the sandwalker.

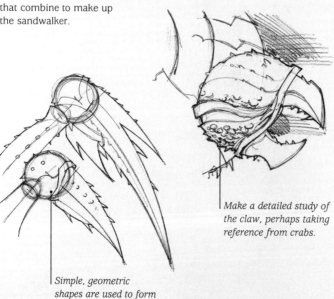

Simple, geometric shapes are used to form the beast's legs.

Make a detailed study of the claw, perhaps taking reference from crabs.

Use a pencil and work from the previously established geometric armature to explore the textures of the armoured legs.

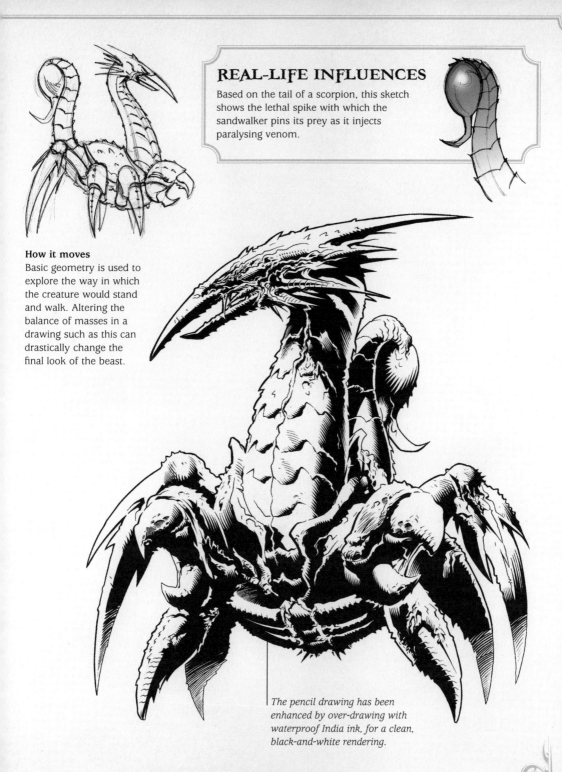

Based on the tail of a scorpion, this sketch shows the lethal spike with which the sandwalker pins its prey as it injects paralysing venom.

How it moves

Basic geometry is used to explore the way in which the creature would stand and walk. Altering the balance of masses in a drawing such as this can drastically change the final look of the beast.

The pencil drawing has been enhanced by over-drawing with waterproof India ink, for a clean, black-and-white rendering.

Now draw your own sandwalkers.

SWAMP BEASTS

Swamps are the hot and sticky breeding grounds of all sorts of creatures. Visit a natural history musem or the hothouse at a botanical garden to get an idea of the inhabitants of this environment. Zoos and aquariums are excellent places to visit to check out real features, such as claws.

Finding inspiration

Amphibians spend part of their time underwater, breathing with gills, and the remainder on land, breathing with lungs. They are cold-blooded, so their body temperature depends on the temperature of their environment.

Snakes are scaly, cold-blooded, egg-laying reptiles. They provide a good resource for creeping, slithering, nonlimbed creatures.

Gharials have great natural features to suit their environment. They differ from crocodiles and alligators due to their long, narrow snout – ideal equipment for seizing fish and frogs underwater. Their hind limbs are paddlelike, and these creatures rarely leave the water, except to nest.

Fig. 1: Frog
Fig. 2: Louisianna
 swamp
Fig. 3: Axolotyl
Fig. 4: Gharial
*Fig. 5: Sternocera
 sternicornis*
Fig. 6: Viper

Use these pages to collect examples of inspiration for swamp beasts, from nature, reference books and the internet. Making notes can help you to recall what it is that drew you to a particular image.

SWAMP ELEMENTAL

The swamp elemental is a powerful spirit that controls its environment and can meld together many natural elements to create a physical form. The creature is difficult to spot because it is made of the same vines and plants as its habitat. Other swamp-dwelling creatures, such as snakes, can get caught up in the swamp elemental's vines; indeed, some favour this habitat as a good source of cover.

This fearsome creature has been coloured in Photoshop, using the Airbrush tool to spray on different layers of colour.

The swamp creature usually emerges very slowly from the waters. Its movement is slow, but its powerful thrashing 'arms' can be very dangerous. It can also change shape quickly and climb trees and other vertical surfaces by 'growing' up them. An unwary traveller could be engulfed by the swamp creature, and sucked down into the swamp to an untimely death.

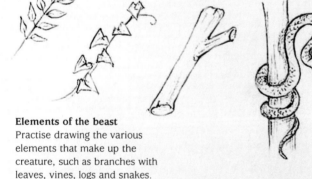

Elements of the beast
Practise drawing the various elements that make up the creature, such as branches with leaves, vines, logs and snakes.

Building up
To compose your swamp elemental, draw the lines of the rough form and then decide where your main vines and branches should go – try to make them fit into the shapes of the creature. Finally, add the details of the smaller vines, leaves and other creatures.

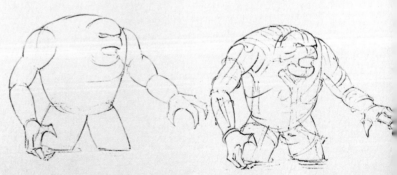

Adding detail
The elemental's mouth and eyes are holes created as the vines recede into the head. The more vines you can wrap around the body, the better.

CREATING THE HAND
Make up the rough skeleton of the hand from branches, and then draw vines and leaves around them to create a three-dimensional form.

Now draw your own swamp elementals.

Imagining the beast
As the creature emerges from the
swamp you begin to see its form.
What looked like rotten foliage
becomes a terrifying beast.

SWAMP DRAGON

The swamp dragon is essentially a giant eel, but it shares characteristics with its dragon relatives, so you can apply the basic principles for creating dragons, as discussed on pages 26–29. This dragon feeds mainly on carrion but will attack and consume live prey in times of extreme hunger.

Throughout the summer months these dragons hibernate, preferring a cooler, damp climate.

Swamp dragons are currently seen as an environmental barometer: because they have a low tolerance for human-made pollution, the presence of a swamp dragon in a location indicates a healthy ecosystem.

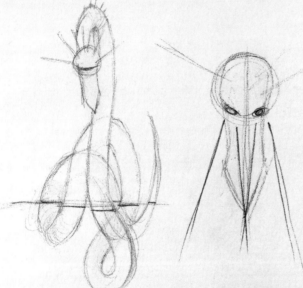

Eye placement
For three-dimensional vision, the eyes have to be set on the front of the head, facing forwards. Fish, with eyes on the sides of their heads, don't see in three dimensions, which is why a fish in a tank can't tell how far away the glass is until it hits it.

Waterline
This construction sketch shows the coils of the body both above and below the water.

Development sketch
This dragon's horns operate like the spines of a porcupine, folding down underwater, and perhaps only becoming erect as a warning to potential enemies.

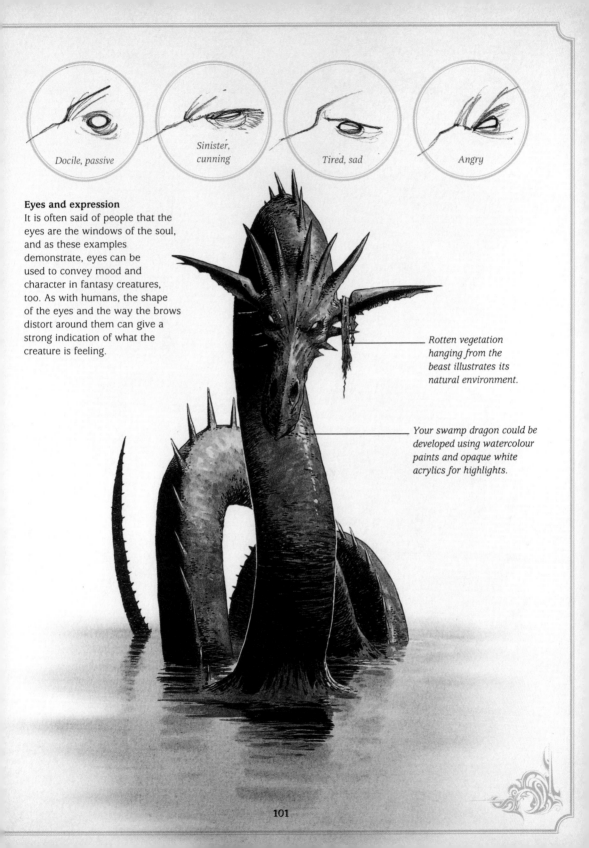

Docile, passive

Sinister, cunning

Tired, sad

Angry

Eyes and expression
It is often said of people that the eyes are the windows of the soul, and as these examples demonstrate, eyes can be used to convey mood and character in fantasy creatures, too. As with humans, the shape of the eyes and the way the brows distort around them can give a strong indication of what the creature is feeling.

Rotten vegetation hanging from the beast illustrates its natural environment.

Your swamp dragon could be developed using watercolour paints and opaque white acrylics for highlights.

Now draw your own swamp dragons.

KROPECHARON

The kropecharon is an insectlike creature, just under 1 metre (3 feet) tall. These arthropods are cunning, but despite their primitive look, they exist in civilised social units. Kropecharons live in tribes, in saltwater mangroves and estuaries, fishing and hunting for survival. They also keep other arthropods, such as crabs and beetles, as livestock, fashioning tools and weapons from their shells.

Ranging from microscopic insects to crustaceans, there are over 1 million known species of arthropods, to provide plenty of inspiration for the imagination. Despite the wide variety of creatures in this family, the bodies of arthropods are remarkably similar. They have a hard body covering, a segmented body and jointed legs, but no backbone. Inspiration for the kropecharon was drawn from several insects. It has features similar to wasps, cockroaches, crickets and the praying mantis. Like most insects, kropecharons are segmented and angular, with a very pointed body shape.

Creating form
To create the kropecharon, begin with simple shapes. These drawings have been rendered digitally, but you can draw the shapes just as well with pencil or pen.

Evolution
Kropecharons can stand upright, despite using their four legs for moving. This posture gives them good balance, while leaving two arms free for using tools.

Having evolved to stand upright, the kropecharon can see over the plants and natural debris that cover its mangrove-swamp habitat.

You can still see the initial shapes in the arthropod's segments.

Shield
Living among mangrove swamps, the kropecharons are able to harvest the bounty of the forests as well as the sea. They use the tough shells of large swamp crabs as shields when hunting even larger land beetles.

Hand
The kropecharon is really a six-legged creature, but the front two legs have evolved to function as hands, able to grasp objects and tools with their two opposable thumbs.

Once you have the basic design for this creature, you could choose to render it digitally, as here. Sketch and paint each segment of the body individually, then assemble for the final image.

Now draw your own kropecharons.

GIANT WORM

The giant worm, like its smaller cousins, feeds on dead and decomposing matter. Perfectly at home in polluted areas, its existence is seen as a prime indicator of an unhealthy environment. A giant worm's life span is measured in geological terms, with specimens predating humans. Traces of giant worms can always be found around mass graves, especially in the fossil record, signifying major extinction events like that of the dinosaurs.

This mutant worm is related genetically to the caterpillar, sharing much of its anatomy, including spinnerets. However, the giant worm doesn't use them to weave a cocoon to enter the chrysalis stage for metamorphosis into a butterfly or moth. The giant worm uses its spinnerets to weave a cocoon for hibernation and to imprison and preserve its prey.

Inspiration sketches
Sketching creatures from nature can give you ideas for movement.

Unfortunately, worms are visually dull, but you can draw reference from other invertebrates such as leeches and caterpillars.

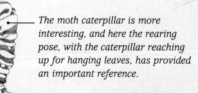

The moth caterpillar is more interesting, and here the rearing pose, with the caterpillar reaching up for hanging leaves, has provided an important reference.

Feeding
The giant worm has hinged mouthparts that surround an open gullet. The appendages operate more like sharp claws than teeth, scooping decaying matter into the worm's mouth for consumption.

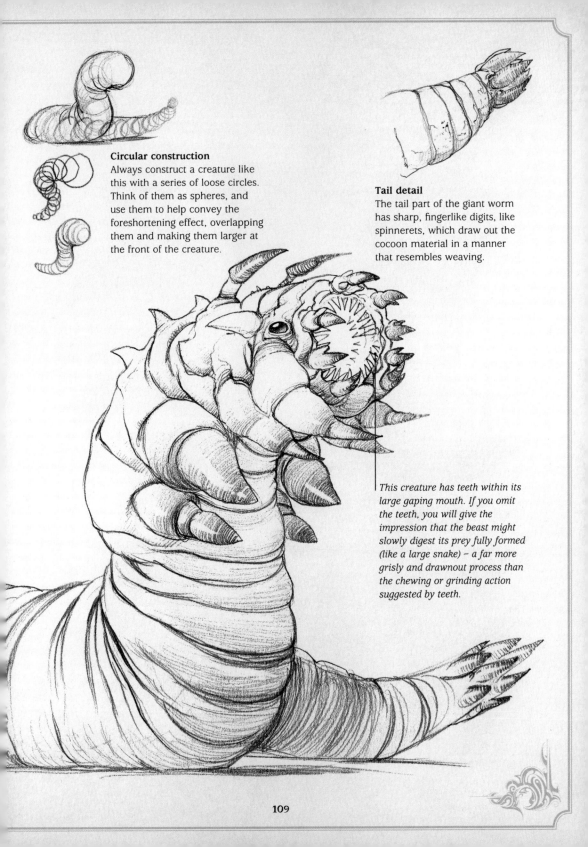

Circular construction
Always construct a creature like this with a series of loose circles. Think of them as spheres, and use them to help convey the foreshortening effect, overlapping them and making them larger at the front of the creature.

Tail detail
The tail part of the giant worm has sharp, fingerlike digits, like spinnerets, which draw out the cocoon material in a manner that resembles weaving.

This creature has teeth within its large gaping mouth. If you omit the teeth, you will give the impression that the beast might slowly digest its prey fully formed (like a large snake) – a far more grisly and drawnout process than the chewing or grinding action suggested by teeth.

Now draw your own giant worms.

SWAMP RAPTOR

Swamp environments present enormous opportunities for the fantasy artist. What may be found lurking in the pool of stagnant water? What mutated monstrosity might lie in wait behind the gnarled trunk of a swamp tree? Only the artist's imagination limits the possibilities when inventing incredible creatures to populate this hostile world.

Real creatures provide a great source of reference and can be combined, distorted and exaggerated to create an endless array of fascinating and potentially lethal monsters with which to inhabit any fantasy scenario. Crocodiles, dragonflies, snakes and any of the other denizens of the swamp can be used as an ideal starting point.

Emphasising physique
This unrefined sketch explores the balance of masses within the creature's physique.

Expression
This experimental sketch of the swamp raptor's head gives it a fierce expression, long tongue and sharp teeth, all of which emphasise its predatory nature.

Experiments with form
Simple geometric forms are used to create a solid base for the drawing. Experimentation with these shapes is always a good idea because the final look of the illustration can be improved dramatically by making small alterations at this stage.

Technique
Use the early stages of working to explore ideas and to push the concept of your creation. Work quickly to play freely with the drawing, and to exploit happy accidents as you scribble; you may inadvertently discover something that takes your creation in an entirely new direction. These initial sketches were executed in broad-tipped marker pen.

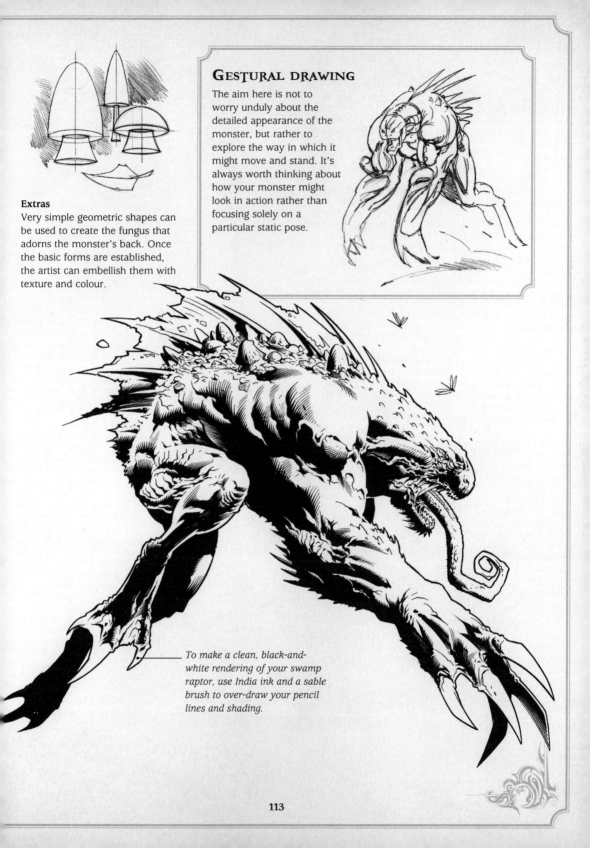

Extras

Very simple geometric shapes can be used to create the fungus that adorns the monster's back. Once the basic forms are established, the artist can embellish them with texture and colour.

GESTURAL DRAWING

The aim here is not to worry unduly about the detailed appearance of the monster, but rather to explore the way in which it might move and stand. It's always worth thinking about how your monster might look in action rather than focusing solely on a particular static pose.

To make a clean, black-and-white rendering of your swamp raptor, use India ink and a sable brush to over-draw your pencil lines and shading.

Now draw your own swamp raptors.

Camouflage
As the swamp raptor waits for
its prey, the moss and toadstools
growing on its back emphasise
the beast's natural camouflage.

FOREST BEASTS

A walk in your local wood or forest could provide natural inspiration for this environment, but for more tropical creatures try reading about the rainforests of Madagascar and the Amazon.

Finding inspiration

A brown bear looks cute and friendly, but don't be fooled. It is a dangerous woodland beast.

Many creatures protect themselves by looking like their environment. Some insects look like leaves, but your fantasy creature could look like a whole tree.

Don't forget to think about where your creature might live or how it looks after its young.

Of course, you don't have to look only at animals. The environment also offers plenty of interesting possibilities to choose from.

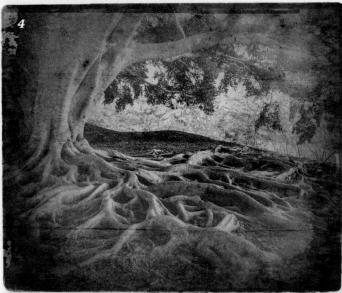

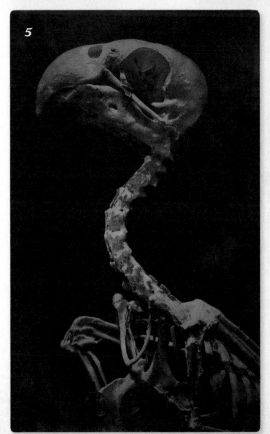

Fig. 1: Brown bear
Fig. 2: Mushrooms
Fig. 3: Lichen
Fig. 4: Tree roots
Fig. 5: Parrot skeleton
Fig. 6: Leaf insect

Gather sources of inspiration for forest beasts here. Collect photos, sketches and notes to help you create your fantasy creatures.

FOREST ELEMENTAL

The forest elemental is wise, quiet and reflective. It is always rooted to the ground – whenever it takes a step, its feet send tendrils into the earth. The elemental is able to change its size and shape, and can grow new bark, foliage and extra limbs when necessary.

As befits a creature of great longevity and thoughtfulness, the forest elemental's strides are extremely slow and deliberate, often causing it to be mistaken for a regular tree. Grass and moss often grow up around its feet while it decides on its next move. But beware any inattentive lumberjack who might try to take an axe to this creature, because, while slow to anger, the forest elemental is quick to strike once it is provoked.

ELEMENTAL FEATURES

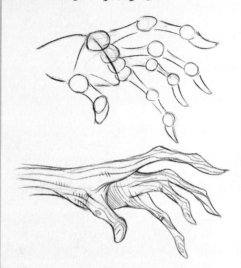

Details such as the long, branchlike fingers, the patches of grass and the roots on the feet can make all the difference when designing an interesting creature. Try to think of features that may surprise and entertain the viewer, as well as be useful or logical for your creature.

Natural studies
Study trees and forests so that you can create believable textures, and practise sketching bark effects.

Musculature
The elemental's limbs are humanlike, so pay attention to real human musculature. Follow the lines of the tree bark and accentuate the muscles, and your creature will appear more realistic.

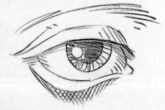

Intelligent eyes
When creating a wise and thoughtful creature, make the eyes as human as possible. This gives viewers something to relate to, immediately enabling them to understand your intended depiction of the character's personality.

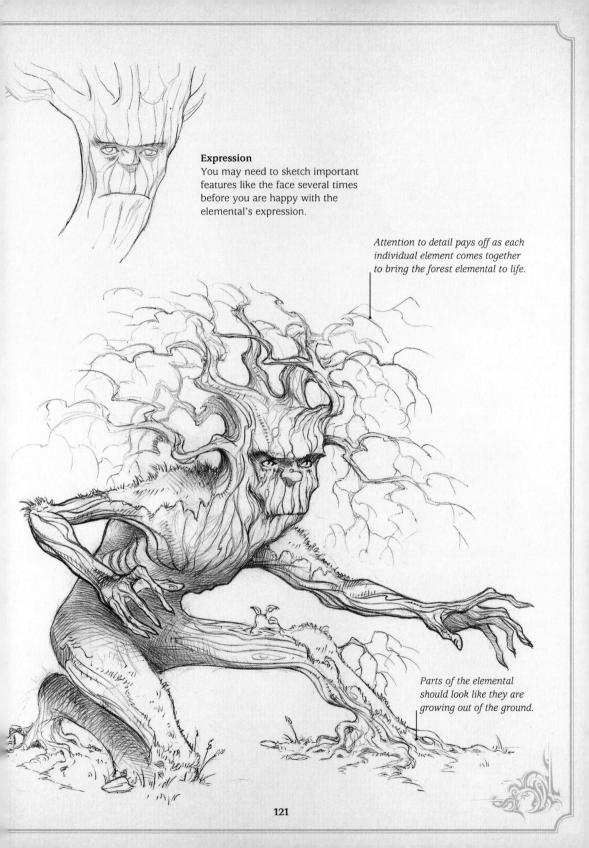

Expression
You may need to sketch important features like the face several times before you are happy with the elemental's expression.

Attention to detail pays off as each individual element comes together to bring the forest elemental to life.

Parts of the elemental should look like they are growing out of the ground.

Now draw your own forest elementals.

Try different expressions for your forest elemental.

FOREST DRAGON

These dragons are limbless and wingless, making them perfectly adapted to life in dense tropical or deciduous forests. Their closest relatives could perhaps be the large constrictor snakes, like the python and boa constrictor. The forest dragon needs to move and hunt in much the same manner.

This dragon has no 'pyrogastric' glands, so it does not breathe fire. Being cold-blooded, it hibernates during the winter months.

Dragon horns

Horns can be mainly for display purposes – attracting a mate, warning off enemies or giving the creature added status within a group. Look at dinosaurs for inspiration. Horns can be any colour the artist chooses, and can even have patterns.

A dragon's horns would probably grow from places where bone was close to the surface of the skin. The shaded areas in this sketch illustrate those places – nose and brow ridges, skull and the heavy part of the jaw towards the back.

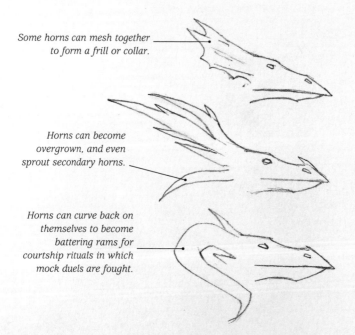

Some horns can mesh together to form a frill or collar.

Horns can become overgrown, and even sprout secondary horns.

Horns can curve back on themselves to become battering rams for courtship rituals in which mock duels are fought.

The number of horns is unimportant – there can be as few or as many as you wish – but always bear in mind that horns have three purposes: attack, defence and display.

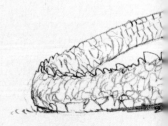

Snakelike form

To create the look of an aggressive forest dragon, draw a coiled tube, which tapers towards the end of the tail. This can be as long and complicated as you wish.

Allow the lines to go through each other, because this helps to link up the coils – unwanted lines can be erased later on.

This dragon looks like a cobra, aggressive and ready for action.

WHY DO HORNS POINT BACKWARDS?

Look at nature to find your answer. Animals with forwards-pointing horns are fewer in number. What kind of animal would charge face first into an enemy, especially a similarly armoured beast? It would risk injuring the very parts – eyes, nose and head – that it seeks to protect.

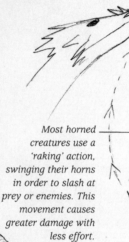

Most horned creatures use a 'raking' action, swinging their horns in order to slash at prey or enemies. This movement causes greater damage with less effort.

Only the larger scales need to be drawn, with the rest shown as short strokes or dashes.

Now draw your own forest dragons.

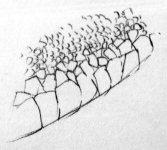

Drawing scales
Drawing scales isn't difficult, but it can be tedious. Often it is best to restrict the fine detail to the part of the beast you wish to use as the focal point, treating the rest in a more impressionistic manner.

RAZORBACK

The razorback is huge, up to 2.5 metres (8 feet) long and weighing 300 kilos (660 pounds). Ferociously territorial and constantly alert, this beast is always ready to defend its family group, and is likely to be found in a powerful stance ready to charge down any intruders.

For telltale signs of the razorback, look out for trampled undergrowth, worn paths through dense forest and loud grunting and smashing sounds. When drawing the beast, try showing some blood around the tusks and mouth, for added effect, or even a snort of steam coming out of its nostrils.

Adapting reality to fantasy
The razorback's hoof very much resembles a pig's trotter, only bigger and with more hair. A pig's trotter is primarily made up of two large modified toes.

Tail detail
The tail is as formidable a weapon as the tusks. It is short and strong with dangerous spikes that can cause massive injuries.

Overlapping circles
The shape of the razorback is made up largely of overlapping circles. Once these are in the correct position, it is just a case of adding in the details. Overlapping shapes give a sense of depth and will help bring your creation to life.

Defining features
The razorback has a boarlike body but takes its name from the three rows of spikes that run the length of its back. The outer spikes are large and flat, protecting the creature from attacks by larger or overhead creatures. The centre row is smaller, and runs directly along the spine.

Tusks
When the razorback lowers its head to charge, the positioning of the sharp tusks and the thick skull at the top of its head ensure that only these areas are exposed, while delicate areas, such as the throat, are protected from harm.

Capturing the head
The head is broad and flat, with a thick skull that protects the razorback from injury when charging its victims. Small beady eyes peer out above massive tusks and teeth. The head of this beast is unusally symmetrical.

At full charge these tusks are easily capable of penetrating armour and impaling enemies.

This beast could be coloured digitally, as here, or painted traditionally.

Now draw your own razorbacks.

CHARACTER SKETCHES

TROLL

Trolls are misshapen and ugly, a fearsome humanoid race from Scandinavian folklore. Traditionally disliking light, they dwell in forests and dark places, and tend to come out only at night. They are voracious and omnivorous eating machines, spending almost all their waking hours searching for and consuming food. Their proportions and gait are similar to those of baboons and orangutans, but they stand much taller, at around 1.8–2.1 metres (6–7 feet). They are rarely portrayed as friendly creatures.

The folklore status of trolls diminished with the advance of Christianity, and they were largely surpassed by more devil-like demons who seemed even more monstrous and destructive. However, that is not to say that they are not still feared by humans.

Exploring an idea
Using the boulder shape as reference, hang limbs off the troll's body until you are happy with the design.

This troll looks as though it could produce great bursts of speed when on all fours.

Here the creature looks like a head only. The arm is too low.

Now the arm is in a better postion, and the leg looks stable.

Now the arms are too high, and there is no space for the ears.

These legs are too straight; this troll would fall over.

Once you have a shape you are happy with, work on the creature's pose.

Drawing the hands

Trolls are not noted for their manual dexterity; any tools this creature might use would be primitive and not very effective. You can, to some extent, use a human hand as a guide to structure, but you might choose to give the hand fewer digits, as shown here.

  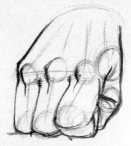

Always start with the most prominent feature, the knuckles, which are positioned on a curve determined by the angle of the hand.

Add the main digits, placing the thumb slightly behind the first finger.

The outlines of the hand and fingers are determined by the thickness of the skin and muscle covering the bones. Avoid straight lines, and exaggerate the curves if you wish to give the impression of fat fingers.

The troll has thick, long hair on its body, and walks using its arms as well as its legs.

Now draw your own trolls.

Ear designs
Experiment until you
find the perfect ears
for your creature.

A troll with these ears
might look too human, and
too comical.

These ears are too
donkeylike. They make the
troll look too sinister.

Too rabbitlike. These
ears make the troll look
too dopey.

SABRE-TOOTHED TREE CAT

With their enormous, deadly, sharp teeth, sabre-toothed tree cats are well known as ferocious predators of prehistoric times. The sabre-toothed cat does not hunt over long distances, preferring to lie in wait and then pounce, throwing itself at its prey, knocking it over and using its teeth to deliver one fatal stab wound to a soft, fleshy area.

The teeth are basically those of large felines, but the same trait appears in several other mammals, such as weasels and bears, so there is plenty of available reference.

This animal is aggressive, so it is important to show it in action. Making it look as though it is about to pounce is a great way to convey its energy.

Head detail
The head and face of a creature are often the focal point of a drawing, so the details need to be worked out quite carefully.

Simple tone can be applied to make the shapes appear more solid, as well as to explore ideas for lighting.

Skull
Think about the structures beneath the skin, and what shapes they might take and why. The big teeth need strong roots!

Choosing a pose
Begin by arranging simple but accurate shapes into a suitably ferocious pose. We rarely see things entirely in profile, and drawing them in this way can make the creature look static and lifeless, so practise drawing from more exciting angles.

Claws
The sabre-toothed cat has serrated
claws to help it climb. This feature
is echoed in the tail blades.

Tail details
The tail is specially adapted to
wrap around branches and dig
into tree limbs to aid climbing.
It also serves as a fearsome
weapon – sharp blades grow out
of the tailbones.

*Repeating a feature, like the blades
on the tail, creates an attractive
pattern, and varying the size adds
visual interest.*

*Giving your creature a
dynamic pose really helps
create that illusion of reality.*

Now draw your own sabre-toothed tree cats.

Real-life inspiration
Making careful
studies from real-life
creatures can help
give your beast
realism and
authenticity.

CENTAUR

Centaurs, a powerful cross between a horse and a human, are mythological creatures with a rather hazy history. Some say they are the offspring of Pegasus, the winged horse, while others believe they were born of Ixion, king of the Lapiths, as a punishment for his murderous and depraved ways. This would explain their savage and mischievous behaviour.

Centaurs are renowned hunters and incredibly fleet of foot. They are nomadic, roaming vast areas of woodland between temporary campsites. These abandoned sites, replete with hoof marks, are usually the first indication of their secretive presence.

The variations in the markings of horses are paralleled in those of a centaur, but dappled varieties are very rare.

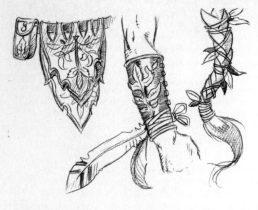

Accessories
Additional detail can make a creature more interesting and tell the viewer something more about it. In the case of the centaur, the use of leather accessories combined with leaves and other plant motifs helps to reinforce the idea that the beast is attuned to nature and a creature of the woods.

Looking down on the centaur can make it appear more vulnerable – perhaps the viewer is high in a tree, about to ambush the unwary creature.

Form
The centaur is a human and horse combined; and to put the two together successfully and create a realistic character, you must become familiar with both forms.

Viewpoint
The angle from which a creature is drawn can alter how we perceive it.

A worm's-eye view can make the figure appear more powerful and imposing.

SENSE OF MOVEMENT

These examples, contrasting hair and accessories in a static pose with those in movement, highlight the way in which you can create greater drama and give the impression of the centaur galloping along.

While sketching you can make changes very easily. Indeed redrawing is an important part of the process. Work up a loose sketch of the whole piece to make sure the key elements are right, before tightening up the detail.

Now draw your own centaurs.

SNOW AND ICE BEASTS

Who knows what may be lurking at the ends of the Earth, or at the top of a snowy mountain? Explorers' travel journals might give you ideas, but nature offers plenty of inspiration for your imagination.

Finding inspiration

Creating white creatures on a white background can be difficult. Look to nature for the textures and colours that can help you.

The Arctic fox has adapted to its home. It can curl up in the snow and keep warm by covering its face with a bushy tail.

Collecting fossils can be a free and fun pastime. Plants and small animals can be found all over the place.

The walrus spends most of its life in the icy waters of the Arctic, but it can be seen on land, too. It has adapted very well to its dual environments. It walks on four legs, while air sacs in its throat enable its head to stay above water. A thick layer of fat keeps it well-insulated from the cold.

Fig. 1: Walrus
Fig. 2: Antarctic ice
Fig. 3: Arctic fox
Fig. 4: Plant fossil
Fig. 5: Polar bear
Fig. 6: Fish fossil

Use these pages to gather together sources of inspiration for snow and ice beasts. You could include references from books, magazines and the internet, as well as your own sketches.

ICE ELEMENTAL

The ice elemental, like the other elementals, is a creature with no physical form of its own, existing as energy and assuming physical form by the manipulation of its environment. It is composed mostly of ice and snow.

The slow-moving ice elemental relies on the rapid melting and refreezing of its physical form for movement. It can be easily outrun by a healthy victim, so it preys instead on unwary and wounded creatures in its environment, lurking in crevasses and around glacial fissures.

Although composed of frozen material (ice water) and essentially a creature of bitter cold, the ice elemental is drawn to heat sources and drains the heat from its victims in order to prolong its own existence. It can thus often be found infesting both subglacial volcanoes and hot springs.

Trying out ideas
The design of a creature that is so abstract is best achieved by an evolving design. Begin with a pencil outline, holding the pencil near the top to give a free, fluid line.

The hunched, crouched shape suggests wariness, something that creeps.

The large roaring head is designed to provoke fear in its victims and is more for effect than purpose.

Work like this until you arrive at a shape you are happy with.

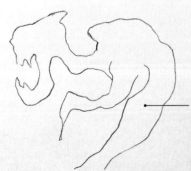

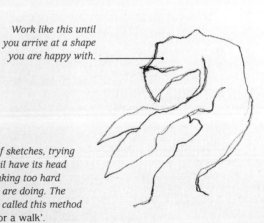

Make a series of sketches, trying to let your pencil have its head rather than thinking too hard about what you are doing. The artist Paul Klee called this method 'taking a line for a walk'.

Developing the head
Work into the pencil outline of the head shape, adding and removing shapes as desired but avoiding overprecise definition.

The shapes reflect the materials the creature is made of – semifluid ice and snow. The teeth, horn and talons resemble icicles, the curve of the back looks like a snow-covered hill and the scaly pattern on the body suggests trodden snow.

For useful reference, look at photographs of wind-sculpted snow and melting ice for the curves.

Now draw your own ice elementals.

ICE DRAGON

Dragons have been part of our folklore for centuries. In fairy tales and legends they are celebrated and feared in equal measure for their astonishing appearance and destructive powers.

Numerous depictions of dragons appear in literature and art, and there are several in this book. You will notice certain characteristics common to most dragons: Wings are commonplace, and they are usually big, but they can be any colour. Most have scales, but some have tough leathery skin; there are big-eared species and small-eared dragons, spiny-backed or smooth and straight, with soft bellies or with horny, all-encompassing carapaces. And, not all dragons breathe fire; this one breathes ice.

Killer tail
It's all in the details, and this spiked tail makes a convincing deadly weapon.

Lizardlike protrusions make your beast look unearthly.

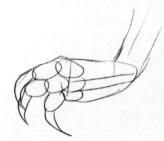

Drawing the claw
The claw is made up of simple shapes and constructional lines.

Dragon's head
The beast has sharp teeth and staring yellow eyes. While these drawings have been rendered digitally, you can practise equally well with pencil or pen.

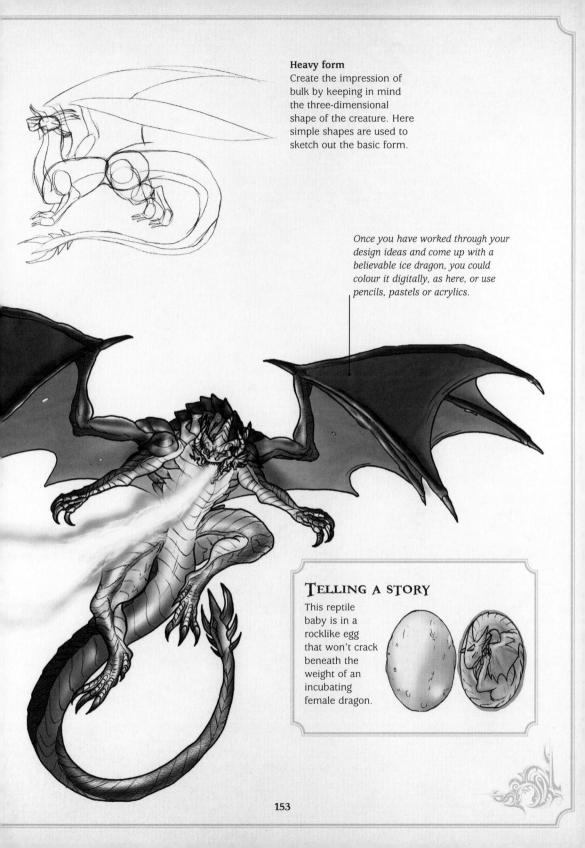

Heavy form
Create the impression of bulk by keeping in mind the three-dimensional shape of the creature. Here simple shapes are used to sketch out the basic form.

Once you have worked through your design ideas and come up with a believable ice dragon, you could colour it digitally, as here, or use pencils, pastels or acrylics.

TELLING A STORY

This reptile baby is in a rocklike egg that won't crack beneath the weight of an incubating female dragon.

Now draw your own ice dragons.

YETI

Otherwise known as the Abominable Snowman, the yeti is a secretive, reclusive, nonaggressive creature that inhabits the mountainous regions of the Himalayas. The beast has been pursued and allegedly sighted by many mountain adventurers over the years. However, no one has managed to secure any real hard evidence for the creature, so perhaps these yeti sightings are better explained by the lack of oxygen at high altitudes, which can cause hallucinations.

Yeti enthusiasts claim that the creature walks upright on two legs, but views differ on its overall appearance. Reported sightings and footprints have suggested that it might be a species of bear or ape as yet undiscovered by humans. Making this yeti a hybrid, with similar characteristics to both bears and apes, covers all eventualities.

Ursine influence
Bears have flat, dense heads with big, thick necks; the torso is usually heavy-set for storing fat during harsh winters.

Physiology
A believable creature is created by making the head half bear and half ape. The body of a polar bear reflects the yeti's icy environment.

General construction
The primitive construction drawing shows the massive shoulder and hip joints where all the creature's main muscle groups are sited. A large, heavy body would be essential for wading through deep drifts of snow. The creature would also need to store an ample amount of fat for hibernation.

Simian influence
The skulls of large apes are similar to the bear's (above), but their heads are much shorter, with a lower-set jaw and no snout.

DRAWING FUR

Pastels and coloured pencils are good fur-drawing tools.

Coloured pencil
This is good for coarse, stiff, longer fur, but is harder to blend than pastel.

Pastel or pastel pencil
This is good for short, soft fur. Rub with a finger or blending stick to soften the lines in places. Add a touch of pale yellow for white fur.

Small eyes make the rest of the head appear larger.

The white fur is short, thick, and greasy, to keep out the cold. White, pale yellow and warm grey pastel pencils have been used here.

Now draw your own yetis.

Sharp teeth
Sharp pointed teeth could make this character seem aggressive and carnivorous, but this yeti is a passive creature.

Flat teeth
Large, flat-topped teeth might make the creature appear too comical. Strike a happy medium between the two extremes.

CREDITS

The material in this book originally appeared in Kev Walker's *Drawing and Painting Fantasy Beasts*.

While every effort has been made to credit contributors, Quarto would like to apologise should there have been any omissions or errors, and would be pleased to make the appropriate correction for future editions of the book.

2happy/shutterstock.com, p68
Andrea Izzotti/shutterstock.com, p45
Anukool Manoton/shutterstock.com, p117
Branislav Zivkovic/shutterstock.com, p117
Choke29/shutterstock.com, p117
Dimos/shutterstock.com, p44
Guraydere/shutterstock.com, p69
I love photo/shutterstock.com, p145
Jacek Jasinski/shutterstock.com, p45
Jaromir Grich/shutterstock.com, p116
John Carnemolla/shutterstock.com, p69
Katrina Outland/shutterstock.com, p44
Kjersti Joergensen/shutterstock.com, p45
Kurit afshen/shutterstock.com, p93
Kyslynkyyhal/shutterstock.com, p92
Lapis2380/shutterstock.com, p93

Michal Ninger/shutterstock.com, p145
Mircea Costina/shutterstock.com, p145
Neil Bromhall/shutterstock,com, p9
Nirandom Tongaroon/Shutterstock.com, p8
Ondrej Prosicky/shutterstock.com, p93
Ramon Carretero/shutterstock.com, p45
Reptiles4all/shutterstock.com, p69
Sergey Uryadnikov/shutterstock.com, p116
Strannick Fox/shutterstock.com, p9
Trevor Fairbank/shutterstock.com, p93
Tryton2011/shutterstock.com, p144
Vaclav Sebek/shutterstock.com, p145
Wildestanimal/shutterstock.com, p44
Yasser El Dershaby/shutterstock.com, p69
Zeljko Radojko/shutterstock.com, p68

The following artists contributed to this book:

Simon Coleby – Sandwalker, Swamp Raptor
Jon Hodgson – Sabre-toothed Tree Cat
Ralph Horsley – Night Elemental, Centaur
Patrick MvEvoy – Sea Elemental, Desert Elemental, Forest Elemental
Lee Smith – Giant Viperfish, Razorback
Anne Stokes – Sphinx, Swamp Elemental
Ruben de Vela – Kraken, Kropecharon, Ice Dragon